Table of contents

Introduction

When I started this journey, I didn't consider myself a writer. I had no literary background or prior experience in publishing. Yet, I've sold over 100,000 copies of my books. How did I do it? By leveraging the most revolutionary technology of our time: artificial intelligence.

This book is more than just the story of my success, it's a practical guide for anyone who wants to embark on a similar journey, without needing to be an expert in writing. I'll show you how I turned a simple idea into a global opportunity by using innovative tools to write, translate, and publish my books.

You'll discover that you don't need to be a creative genius or have endless resources to become a successful author. What you do need is a clear strategy, the courage to experiment, and a willingness to embrace change.

Within these pages, you'll find my secrets, the techniques I've refined, the mistakes I've made, and the lessons I've learned. Whether your goal is to write for passion, earn extra income, or build a full-time career, this book will provide you with the tools to start and thrive.

Scattered throughout this book are 18 valuable secrets, insights you should commit to memory if you aspire to succeed in this field. These are 18 pearls of wisdom I've collected over the years that helped me achieve success as an author, despite not being a "writer" in the traditional sense, and sell over 100,000 copies.

It doesn't matter where you start. If you have a story to tell and the right mindset, success is within your reach. Now, let's dive in together and explore how to turn ideas into books and books into extraordinary achievements.

Chapter 1 - 100,000 books sold

When we think of a successful writer, we often imagine someone spending years meticulously crafting every word to create a masterpiece. My story, however, is entirely different. I'm not a writer in the traditional sense, and I've never considered myself particularly creative. Yet, I achieved a dream that many writers chase for a lifetime: selling 100,000 copies of my books.

How did I do it? Not through innate literary talent or deep expertise in countless subjects. My secret? A modern, unexpected ally: artificial intelligence.

I was just an ordinary person with a regular job and modest satisfaction. Writing became less of a passion and more of a necessity, a way to build an alternative source of income. My entry into the world of writing was gradual. At first, I wrote articles for my websites on various topics. My style was just adequate for my needs, and I never aspired to become a novelist or take writing classes. My skills remained functional but unpolished.

My first book

The idea for my first book happened almost by chance. While browsing online, I stumbled upon an article about self-publishing on Amazon. After researching the topic, I realized it was entirely possible to publish a book independently without relying on traditional publishers. So, I sat down at my computer and started writing.

What was it about? That I won't reveal, I prefer to remain anonymous and leave you guessing who I might be and what books I've written (the name on the cover, of course, is a pseudonym).

Think of this book as a lottery ticket. I found a method to succeed (and it worked), and now I want to share it. I believe luck should be shared with those willing to take a chance. When I wrote my first book, AI tools didn't exist, so I had to do everything on my own. It took me an entire year, a timeframe that felt quick at the time but now seems painfully slow.

When the book was finished, I faced the next challenge: the cover. Lacking design skills, I turned to a website that delivered a professional cover in just three days for a modest fee. I created an Amazon profile, followed a few tutorials, and within a week, my book was online, ready for purchase and print. The result? About 400 copies sold over three years. Back then, it felt like a lot, but now I realize it was a modest start.

Secret 1: this book is short (and deliberately so)

I could have written hundreds of pages, but I chose to keep it concise, practical, and to the point. Why? To save you from lengthy, repetitive content and provide only what you truly need: clear, actionable advice. My goal is simple: to offer you a straightforward guide that equips you in just a few hours to jumpstart your journey into publishing and create your first successful book.

The shift to artificial intelligence

My first book showed me that I could write and self-publish, but turning this into a profitable career required speeding up the process. Writing the book was the bottleneck, and artificial intelligence became the key to accelerating everything.

When I discovered the potential of AI, I asked myself, "Why not let a machine write the books while I focus on choosing topics and organizing ideas?" That's when I began creating books on trending subjects and translating them into multiple languages without needing to learn them.

My first experiment

My first experiment with AI felt like a game. I chose ChatGPT, mainly out of convenience, and decided to tackle a practical and popular topic: a personal productivity guide. I didn't have specific expectations, I was just curious to see if it would work.

In just a few days, I had a complete draft. AI helped me generate content, structure the book, and even suggest catchy titles. With minimal time and money invested, my first AI-assisted book was ready.

The first sale and a new idea

When the first sale came through, I felt a mix of amazement and satisfaction. Someone had bought my book! That's when I realized that if I could replicate this process, AI could be the key to creating books on diverse topics in multiple languages.

Over the following months, I continued writing and exploring different themes. I discovered that the real secret lay in choosing the right topics and tailoring the style for various audiences.

Toward 100,000 copies sold

Each new book was an opportunity, not just to earn money but to refine my approach. At first, sales were slow, but as my catalog grew and translations reached new markets, the numbers began to climb.

Selling 100,000 copies wasn't an overnight success. I studied market trends and optimized my strategy. Despite having limited writing experience and no knowledge of foreign languages, AI gave me access to a global market and helped me establish a presence as an author.

A new kind of writer

I became a different kind of writer, one who leverages technology to expand their capabilities. Instead of spending years on a single manuscript, I produce targeted content designed for a global audience. Thanks to AI, I've proven that you don't need to be a literary expert to sell books; what truly matters is understanding your audience and using the right tools.

This book is my manual, a guide for anyone who wants to follow this path and transform writing into a dynamic, modern career.

Secret 2: you don't need to be a writer or a polyglot

Don't worry if you're not a skilled writer or fluent in multiple languages. With AI, you can create high-quality books without limitations. Let your imagination soar and think big, these innovative tools provide everything you need to turn your ideas into books, one after another.

Chapter 2 - Artificial Intelligence as a writing companion

When I first started using artificial intelligence for writing, I approached it with a mix of skepticism and curiosity. How could a machine possibly support the creative process of writing? I didn't consider myself an expert with words, let alone an author. Yet, I quickly realized that AI could do far more than I had imagined, helping me create content efficiently and effectively.

Choosing the right platform

The first step was finding the right platform. Today, there are plenty of options, each with unique features.

When I started, choices were limited, and, true to my naturally lazy tendencies, I didn't spend too much time experimenting. After a few trials, I found ChatGPT, and it quickly became my AI of choice. It was like love at first sight, a true spark of connection.

That said, today's landscape offers many alternatives. Different platforms provide various customization options: some let you select the tone, adjust chapter lengths, or decide between formal and conversational language. It's essential to experiment and figure out which platform best suits your needs and audience. For instance, I discovered that practical, instructional topics resonate better with an approachable tone, while technical subjects require a more professional style.

Overcoming writer's block

One of the most surprising benefits of AI was how it helped me overcome the dreaded writer's block. In the past, I had plenty of ideas but struggled to put them into words. Every time I sat down to write, I felt stuck, unable to start. AI became invaluable in breaking through that barrier: all it needed was a prompt, a basic idea, and it would generate a first draft.

While the initial output wasn't perfect, it provided a starting point that freed my creativity to take over.

When tackling lengthy projects or maintaining a steady writing pace, AI also helped manage the workload without sacrificing quality. This became especially critical as I began publishing regularly. No longer did I need to spend days wrestling with a blank page. Instead, I could focus on refining the content and exploring the best topics.

If you're unsure about choosing a subject, structuring chapters, or developing ideas, just ask your "friend" ChatGPT. It's like magic, problems dissolve, and solutions appear.

Creating high-quality content

Some people assume that AI produces cold, mechanical text. While it's true that AI can sound impersonal without guidance, the secret lies in knowing how to direct it. Simply giving it a topic and expecting perfection won't work. Clear instructions, consistent feedback, and thorough editing are essential.

For example, I've learned that providing a detailed structure, such as a list of key points or a logical sequence, leads to better results. If I'm writing a manual, I break the subject into chapters or sections and specify what I want in each part. This level of precision dramatically improves the final output.

I never settle for the first draft. After receiving a draft from AI, I review it carefully and make the necessary adjustments, reorganizing paragraphs, adding examples, or rewriting sentences for clarity. While AI is an incredible assistant, the final human touch remains vital to give the text personality.

Sometimes, after making my revisions, I feed the updated version back into the AI for further refinement. This iterative process results in richer, more polished content. It's a game-changer!

Treating AI like a true collaborator, engaging with it as you would with a real person, makes all the difference. Initially, it might feel odd to ask questions naturally, but it quickly becomes second nature. Before you know it, you'll feel like you have a new work partner, always ready to help and offer solutions when you're stuck.

With AI by your side, writer's block becomes a thing of the past.

Secret 3: treat AI as a knowledgeable collaborator

Think of AI as a human partner and communicate with it in a way that feels natural to you. Prefer formal language? Go for it. Prefer a more casual tone? That works too, AI will understand either way. Over time, you'll develop your own style for interacting with it and getting the best results.

Most importantly, share all your thoughts, even the unpolished ones. If you can't find the right words, don't worry. Write down whatever comes to mind, AI will organize and clarify your ideas, turning them into a coherent and well-structured text.

Customizing tone and voice

One of the most fascinating aspects of using AI is the ability to customize the tone and voice of my books. I didn't want all my books to sound the same or feel "robotic." I discovered that I could instruct AI to adopt a conversational or formal tone depending on my target audience.

For instance, if I'm writing about meditation techniques for beginners, I ask AI to use simple and reassuring language. On the other hand, if I'm creating a guide on corporate productivity strategies, I prefer a more authoritative and direct tone. This flexibility has allowed me to cater to a diverse range of readers, creating content that truly resonates with them.

Most writers develop a consistent style that makes them recognizable, but this can limit their appeal to a wider audience. Even the most celebrated authors have readers who adore them and others who don't connect with their style. AI, however, enables you to tailor your tone for each subject and audience, crafting books on different topics with styles that resonate perfectly with specific readers.

Secret 4: match the tone to your book's theme and audience

Choose the right tone for each book based on its subject and intended readers. A conversational tone works well for practical or introductory topics, while a more formal, professional style suits specialized guides. Adapting your tone will make your message resonate better with readers, making each book more engaging and effective.

Using AI to amplify creativity

Ultimately, I've learned that AI isn't a replacement for creativity, it's an amplifier. Without a solid idea or clear direction, AI tends to produce generic content. But when I provide a well-thought-out outline and guide it with intent, it becomes an incredibly powerful tool.

Thanks to AI, I've been able to explore topics I never thought I'd tackle and do so in a fraction of the time it would've taken me to write alone. It's like having a tireless collaborator ready to turn my ideas into reality. There's no greater satisfaction than seeing a project take shape and knowing you've created something you might not have had the time or skills to achieve otherwise.

Adapting and innovating

AI is an ever-evolving field, and I've had to adapt along the way. Platforms continuously improve, introducing new features and refining the quality of their outputs. Staying updated and embracing these advancements is essential. AI isn't static, and neither is the way I use it.

This dynamic approach has allowed me to move beyond generic topics and create targeted, relevant content for a growing audience. Through it all, AI has become an indispensable partner, helping me turn my passion into a thriving career.

Chapter 3 - Finding winning topics

One of the most critical aspects of succeeding as an author, especially when using artificial intelligence, is choosing the right topic. Writing a book, even with the help of our virtual assistant, still requires time and resources, so it's essential to focus on subjects that not only capture a broad audience's interest but also have strong sales potential. For me, selecting the right topics has become a well-honed strategy, a systematic process to identify themes that resonate with readers.

This step is vital and deserves your time and attention. Writing a book, as you've likely realized by now, is straightforward: you can easily create professional and engaging covers, publish the book, and reach readers worldwide. However, the key to maximizing your efforts lies in selecting topics that truly resonate with your audience. After all, what's the point of writing a book that no one wants to read?

Start with the audience's needs

My first rule is always to begin with the audience's needs. What problems do they want to solve? What questions do they frequently ask? The key to success is understanding what people are truly looking for and offering them a book that provides value and practical solutions.

To do this, I explore various tools and resources. I read online news to identify trending topics or emerging themes. I conduct keyword research to understand where public interest is heading. Another invaluable resource is analyzing best-selling books. Most book-selling platforms provide bestseller lists, which offer insights into the most in-demand topics.

Each country is a unique market, and I don't limit myself to my home country. Expanding to new markets can reveal untapped pools of readers. With today's translation capabilities, writing books in nearly any language is now a realistic opportunity.

This research technique is particularly useful for brainstorming ideas. It opens my eyes to topics I knew little or nothing about, allowing me to reach audiences I wouldn't have otherwise considered. Time spent analyzing bestseller trends is among my best investments. Interestingly, successful topics vary greatly depending on the country. This allows me to maximize sales across different markets. For example, if I identify a popular topic in Japan, I can easily translate it into other languages. Even if it doesn't become a hit elsewhere, it often generates some sales, and sometimes, a seemingly unpromising topic in one market turns out to be an unexpected winner in another.

Secret 5: diversify topics by starting with different countries

To achieve consistent, high-quality results, try choosing

each new topic by starting with a different country. For instance, today, identify the hottest topic in England, write a book on it, and translate it into the languages you want. Next month, explore trends in Brazil, create a book on that subject, and translate it again into various languages. Repeat this process each month, starting with a new country and publishing in the local language. This approach allows you to tap into global interests while keeping your content fresh and varied.

Finding profitable niches

One of my most important discoveries was the existence of "profitable niches." These are specific topics that may not attract massive audiences but still have a dedicated group of passionate readers. Focusing on broad topics can make it harder to stand out because competition is fierce. By targeting smaller niches, you have a better chance of reaching an engaged, enthusiastic audience.

For example, a general topic like "productivity" might be highly competitive. But narrowing it down to "productivity for freelancers" or "productivity for working moms" allows you to offer tailored content that addresses specific needs. This approach has enabled me to write books with a clearly defined audience, creating a direct connection with readers who feel the book was made just for them.

One fascinating aspect of niches is how easily they foster reader loyalty. Once you've identified a profitable niche and published a successful book, you can use that success to build a lasting relationship with your audience. Over time, you can write a second book on the same topic, adding new insights and details to keep readers engaged. Those who enjoyed the first book will eagerly purchase the new one, knowing it will provide even more value.

Secret 6: alternate between broad topics and niche subjects

To maximize sales, alternate between books on broad-interest topics and niche subjects. Books targeting large audiences have the potential to reach many readers but face stiff competition. Niche topics, on the other hand, attract smaller audiences with less competition. If your book resonates, you can build a loyal customer base eagerly awaiting your next release on the same subject.

Keep in mind that niche sizes vary by country. A topic considered niche in one market might be mainstream in another, or completely irrelevant elsewhere. For example, a book on high-altitude skiing won't find readers in a country without mountains or ski culture.

The "problem-solving formula"

Another key criterion I use for choosing topics is the "problem-solving formula." Books that offer practical, concrete solutions to common problems tend to perform well, especially in self-help, personal growth, or how-to genres. Many readers are searching for solutions to everyday challenges, from organizing their lives to improving their finances, managing stress, or taking care of their health.

This formula was particularly helpful in my early days

when I needed topics with broad appeal. Before writing a book, I always ask myself one crucial question: "What problem am I solving for my reader?" If I can identify a clear and compelling answer, I know I'm on the right track.

Monitoring market trends

Market trends are another essential tool. There are times when certain topics become especially popular, often due to a new movie, cultural phenomenon, or social or technological shift. Keeping an eye on trends allows me to tap into current conversations and respond to emerging interests.

To track trends, I use tools like Google Trends, social media platforms, and news services to identify rising topics. Acting quickly is key when you spot a trend, as the window of opportunity is often short. Thanks to AI, I can rapidly generate high-quality content and publish my book in record time, capitalizing on the trend while it's still hot.

Secret 7: speed is crucial for trending topics

When writing books on trending topics, speed is everything. Trends fade quickly, so as soon as you spot a subject gaining attention in news articles, TV programs, websites, or social media, aim to publish your book within a week. Being the first to cover a new topic positions you as an authority and earns you valuable mentions in articles and posts by others.

Even if the trend lasts only a few months, you'll have maximized the moment, sold a significant number of copies, and be ready to move on to the next big topic.

Experimenting with different topics

Not all my books have been successful. I've written about topics I thought had great potential but ended up underperforming. However, this trial-and-error process has been invaluable in helping me understand the market and refine my ability to pick winning topics.

Whenever a book doesn't meet expectations, I analyze reader feedback, reviews, and what might have gone wrong. Sometimes it's a matter of timing; other times, it's the title or how I described the content. This ongoing experimentation has taught me to make better decisions and quickly recognize topics with strong potential.

Secret 8: experiment boldly and embrace failure

Have the courage to experiment and don't fear failure. You're exploring uncharted territory without established studies or best practices to rely on. Learn from your mistakes: take notes and reflect on both the books that sell thousands of copies and those that sell only a few (trust me, you'll have some of these too). Every experience, positive or negative, is a valuable lesson to improve.

Secret 9: repackage books that didn't sell

If a book hasn't sold well after a couple of years, don't discard all your hard work. Instead, analyze what went wrong: Was it the topic, cover, title, length, or something else? Once you've pinpointed the issue, consider reworking the book using AI. Add new chapters, reorganize the structure, and enrich the content with at least 50 additional pages. Change the title and cover, then relaunch it. You might be surprised at the fresh and positive results this "repurposing" can achieve.

Building a system for topic selection

Over time, I've developed a framework to help me systematically choose book topics. It revolves around three simple questions:

1. Does the topic interest enough people?

2. Is there already a lot of content on this subject, or is there room for a new perspective?

3. Does the topic solve a specific problem or meet a clear need?

If the answer to all three is "yes," the topic has strong potential. This framework helps me filter ideas and focus only on projects likely to succeed.

Preparing research for artificial intelligence

After selecting the topic, I focus on gathering all the necessary material to provide the AI with a solid foundation to work from. The research phase is essential: a well-prepared AI produces more coherent and useful content for the reader. Although AI can generate content, it is crucial to provide clear guidelines and a strong starting point.

I collect articles, studies, guides, and other relevant

information. This allows me to clearly outline the direction to follow and the key concepts to develop. It's like giving instructions to a collaborator: the clearer the instructions, the better the results will be.

This is a critical step: don't expect AI to do all the work on its own. While it might be capable, the outcome wouldn't be optimal. To produce high-quality books, your human input is indispensable. Relying entirely on AI rarely leads to lasting success. That's why experimenting is useful to understand both the strengths and limitations of your artificial "collaborator." At the same time, identify your own strengths and weaknesses. A winning alliance between human and machine maximizes the strengths of both and mitigates their weaknesses, creating a truly effective combination.

Choosing the right theme is, for me, the first step toward success. Having a vague idea is not enough; a precise strategy is required, supported by data, careful market analysis, and the ability to meet the audience's needs. Thanks to this approach, I have developed a real "sensitivity" for topics that can sell, and I have learned to trust my method.

AI is a powerful tool, but without a solid research foundation and an understanding of audience needs, it risks producing content that fails to capture interest. This chapter serves as an invitation to anyone embarking on this journey: don't be afraid to dedicate time to selecting the right theme. It is the fundamental element on which to build a book that not only attracts readers but also truly meets their expectations.

Chapter 4 - Writing for a global audience

When I began writing and publishing books with the help of artificial intelligence, one of my main goals was to reach as wide an audience as possible. We live in a globalized world where readers can be found anywhere on the planet, speaking different languages. To take advantage of this opportunity, I decided to translate my books into the major international languages. But how could I do that without knowing those languages? Once again, artificial intelligence came to my rescue, allowing me to translate my books and make them accessible worldwide.

The power of automated translations

One of the most surprising discoveries I made was the quality achieved by AI-powered translation platforms. Initially, I worried that an automated translation might feel cold or inaccurate, potentially alienating readers. However, I quickly realized that, with the right tools and minimal revisions, it's possible to produce fluid and professional translations.

Using AI for translations saved me both time and

money. Hiring a human translator can be expensive, especially when publishing books in multiple languages. With AI translation platforms, I was able to make my content available in English, Spanish, French, German, Japanese, and many other languages without requiring a large budget.

Choosing which languages to translate into

The choice of languages wasn't random. First, I studied the global book market to identify languages that could reach a broad and interested audience. English, Spanish, French, German, and Italian were obvious choices due to the large number of readers speaking these languages and their widespread use across many countries. Later, I added other languages with strong market potential, like Portuguese for Brazil and Japanese for the Asian market.

Whenever I decide to translate a new book, I ask myself: "In which language is this most likely to succeed?" I analyze sales trends in different countries and determine if the book's topic holds particular cultural relevance in specific regions. For example, if I'm writing a book about productivity and know there's strong interest in Japan for that subject, Japanese becomes a priority for translation.

Optimizing translations

To achieve effective translations with AI, it's crucial to start with clear and simple text. I've found that direct writing with short sentences and accessible language makes the AI's job easier, resulting in more accurate translations. I avoid overly idiomatic expressions or culturally specific phrases that could be misinterpreted or lead to poor-quality translations.

After completing a translation, I review the text carefully

to ensure it reads smoothly and naturally. I often use a double-checking method: translating the text back into the original language. For example, if I translate a book from English to Spanish, I'll retranslate the Spanish version back into English to confirm that the concepts remain consistent. While this extra step takes time, it's especially helpful for languages with grammatical structures different from the original text.

If I'm unsure about a translation's quality, I sometimes use human editing services to review key sections while keeping costs low. This combination of automated translations and human review has allowed me to achieve high-quality results with minimal investment.

Navigating cultural challenges

Translation also means adapting the content to the target culture. What works in one country might not be as effective in another. For instance, I've learned that certain self-help or personal productivity topics popular in Western countries need a different approach for an Asian audience, where cultural expectations and sensitivities may vary.

That's why I always do some cultural research before launching a translation in a new language. In some cases, it's helpful to adjust examples or metaphors, or to include a brief introduction explaining how the book fits the target culture. This extra effort can significantly improve how the book is received.

Managing global reader expectations

One of my initial concerns was how native readers would perceive a book translated with AI. Would they notice a difference compared to one translated by a professional? Fortunately, translation platforms have improved greatly, and by following the optimization techniques I've described, the results have been overwhelmingly positive.

Readers also appreciate having access to content in their own language, even if it's not 100% perfect. Often, what matters most to them is the substance, the ability to find answers and solutions. Many have even written to thank me for making my books available in their language, which has motivated me to keep going.

To minimize issues and ensure accurate translations, I carefully select both the topics and writing styles. Typically, I focus on manuals or guides with specific content, where the primary goal is to provide clear information rather than artistic expression. For this reason, I avoid novels or works where idiomatic expressions play a critical role. Writing a novel requires meticulous attention to the nuance of every sentence, as the way it's phrased can change the entire message. In manuals, however, clarity and effectiveness are the primary concerns.

Selecting markets for distribution

Publishing in multiple languages has opened the door to various markets. Every self-publishing platform offers the opportunity to release books in different languages and reach readers worldwide.

I analyze sales to identify which markets respond best to specific languages and adjust my strategy accordingly. If I notice a book performs well in a particular language, I might invest more in promoting it in that region or write another book on a similar topic tailored to that audience. This flexibility allows me to focus on what works, increasing my chances of success.

Secret 10: optimize your advertising investment

Analyzing a market allows you to target and optimize your advertising spend. If a topic proves highly popular in a particular country, allocate the advertising budget for that book primarily in that nation. Of course, translate the book into other languages since the primary work is already done, but avoid investing in promotions where results are likely to be limited.

A continuous learning experience

Using AI translations has enabled me to reach readers worldwide, but it's also been a continuous learning experience. I've had to refine my approach, discover new techniques, and adapt to feedback. Publishing in multiple languages has transformed my perspective: I'm no longer writing for a local market, but for a global audience. Every book I release gives me the chance to improve, to better understand what international readers are looking for, and to adapt to their needs.

AI has made what was once unthinkable for an independent author possible: reaching a global audience, selling books in multiple languages, and building an international presence without being a polyglot or a translation expert.

This chapter is an encouragement for anyone dreaming of reaching beyond borders, without the limitations of language or geography. AI translation isn't perfect, but with the right tools and a little effort, you can achieve high-quality results and win readers around the world. My experience has taught me that with a clear strategy and attention to cultural specifics, you can open the doors to unexpected markets and build a global readership that transcends linguistic barriers.

Chapter 5 - Analyzing international book markets

The global publishing industry is a dynamic and growing sector, with key markets distinguished by their number of readers, revenue, and reading preferences. With the expansion of digital publishing, book consumption has increased in many countries, diversifying genres and formats. Here's a closer look at some of the world's major book markets.

1. United States

The United States boasts one of the largest and most dynamic book markets globally, with over 800 million books sold annually and revenues exceeding $30 billion.

- Readers: about 75% of adults read at least one book a year, with digital formats accounting for 25% of sales.
- Top categories: popular genres include fiction, self-help, business and personal development, and young adult literature. Thrillers and fantasy, in particular, dominate the entertainment fiction market.

- Trends: audiobooks are experiencing explosive growth, with a year-over-year increase of 30%, making them the fastest-growing format.

2. China

China ranks as the second-largest book market globally, with annual sales exceeding $25 billion.

- Readers: around 60% of the population reads regularly, with a strong preference for print books, though the digital market is growing, especially among younger readers.
- Top categories: nonfiction genres, including history, philosophy, and social sciences, dominate, alongside contemporary Chinese fiction. The educational sector, driven by a large student population, is particularly robust.
- Trends: online reading platforms for serialized web novels have surged in popularity, creating a thriving parallel industry.

3. Germany

Germany leads the European book market, with annual revenues surpassing $10 billion.

- Readers: about 68% of adults read at least one book a year, with a strong attachment to traditional reading. E-books account for just 5% of total sales.
- Top categories: fiction, particularly crime and thriller genres, leads sales, followed by nonfiction in psychology, philosophy, and sciences.
- Trends: audiobooks are gaining traction, especially among young adults. Germany is also a pioneer in sustainable publishing, focusing on eco-friendly printing.

4. United Kingdom

The UK is one of the oldest and most established book markets, valued at approximately $8 billion annually.

- Readers: over 70% of the population reads at least one book a year. Audiobooks are particularly popular, with sustained growth in recent years.
- Top categories: fiction, especially thrillers and historical novels, as well as cookbooks and lifestyle titles. Self-help and wellness books also have a strong market presence.
- Trends: children's and young adult books, including illustrated titles and graphic novels, are rapidly growing in popularity.

5. Japan

Japan's unique book market is defined by its strong affinity for manga and illustrated narratives, with annual revenues around $6 billion.

- Readers: nearly 90% of young adults read manga or graphic novels, while traditional book readership remains steady.
- Top categories: manga dominates, followed by short novels and contemporary Japanese fiction. Self-help and personal development books are also popular.
- Trends: digital manga and book consumption via smartphones are rapidly increasing, especially among younger generations.

6. France

France's book market generates about $5 billion annually, with a deeply ingrained reading culture.

- Readers: approximately 75% of French adults read at least one book a year, with a strong preference for printed books. E-books account for only a small percentage of sales.
- Top categories: fiction, especially French and contemporary literature, along with political essays and historical novels.
- Trends: growing interest in ecology and sustainability-themed books, as well as graphic novels and bandes dessinées, which attract a broad audience.

7. Italy
Italy's book market, valued at around $3 billion, is slowly growing, driven by cultural initiatives and reading incentives.

- Readers: about 40% of the population reads at least one book a year, with a preference for print books.
- Top categories: contemporary Italian fiction, thrillers, and self-help books are the most popular. Children's and young adult literature is also gaining traction.
- Trends: audiobooks and e-books are growing, particularly among younger audiences. Historical fiction and nonfiction are also seeing increased interest.

8. Spain
Spain is a major Spanish-language book market, valued at approximately $2 billion.

- Readers: around 60% of the population reads at least one book a year, with a rising preference for e-books, particularly in urban areas.
- Top categories: fiction, especially thrillers and

contemporary Spanish literature, dominates sales. Self-help, personal development, and children's literature are also highly popular.

- Trends: audiobooks are increasingly in demand, especially among commuters. Regional languages like Catalan, Galician, and Basque are also seeing growing interest, reflecting Spain's cultural diversity.

9. Brazil

As South America's largest book market, Brazil's industry is valued at $1.5 billion, though it faces economic challenges.

- Readers: about 50% of Brazilians read at least one book a year. The market is evenly split between print and digital, with digital gaining traction among young adults.
- Top categories: fiction, particularly Brazilian and international bestsellers, dominates. Religious and spiritual books, especially evangelical and self-help titles, are also very popular.
- Trends: government initiatives to promote reading have supported the industry, with growing interest in local literature and international translations. E-books and audiobooks are becoming more popular, fueled by increasing mobile access.

10. Canada

Canada's bilingual book market, driven by English and French-speaking populations, is worth over $1.6 billion annually.

- Readers: around 70% of Canadians read at least one book a year, with a strong preference for printed books,

though digital formats are gaining popularity, especially among younger readers.
- Top categories: fiction leads sales, followed by nonfiction in history, psychology, and current events. Canadian literature and children's books are also highly appreciated.
- Trends: audiobooks are rapidly expanding, particularly in urban areas, while demand for French-language content continues to grow in francophone regions.

11. India
The book market in India is among the largest in the world, experiencing significant growth due to its vast young population. The estimated market value is around $7 billion, making it one of the leading emerging markets.

- Readers: approximately 50% of the population reads regularly, with a strong preference for printed books, although digital formats are gaining traction, especially among the youth.
- Top categories: educational and academic books dominate the market, followed by novels, contemporary Indian fiction, and self-help books.
- Trends: the increasing accessibility of smartphones has driven the growth of e-books and audiobooks. Web novels are also gaining popularity among younger readers.

12. Australia
Australia has a medium-sized yet highly active publishing market, with an annual revenue of approximately $2 billion.

- Readers: about 65% of Australians read at least one book per year, with a strong preference for printed books, though digital formats are on the rise.

- Top categories: fiction, particularly crime and thriller genres, is highly popular, followed by cookbooks and wellness books. Contemporary Australian literature also enjoys a strong following.

- Trends: audiobooks are rapidly growing in popularity, as is interest in children's fiction. Books by local authors are especially well-regarded.

13. Mexico

Mexico is one of the leading Spanish-language publishing markets, with an estimated value of around $1 billion. Despite economic challenges, the publishing sector remains well-established.

- Readers: around 45% of the population reads regularly, with a preference for printed books.

- Top categories: fiction (particularly thrillers and historical novels) leads the market, followed by self-help, religion and spirituality, and children's fiction.

- Trends: in recent years, demand for e-books and audiobooks has increased, especially among younger generations. Comics and graphic novels are also gaining momentum, driven by their popularity among young adults.

14. Russia

Russia has a well-established publishing market, with an annual revenue of approximately $1.5 billion. Despite economic and political challenges, Russia's literary tradition continues to support a vibrant market.

- Readers: around 50% of the population reads at least one book per year, with a preference for physical books, though digital formats are becoming more popular.

- Top categories: russian and international fiction, especially classics, are very popular, along with historical novels and nonfiction in fields such as psychology and philosophy.

- Trends: e-books are growing in popularity, and the audiobook sector is expanding. Translations of international bestsellers and works by local authors continue to dominate sales.

Key insights for global authors

Every book market has its unique traits, shaped by cultural traditions, reading habits, and available technologies. Established markets like the United States, China, and Germany remain leaders, while emerging markets such as India, Brazil, and Mexico are gaining traction thanks to a growing interest in reading and increased access to new technologies.

Understanding these markets is essential for authors aiming to reach international audiences. Differences in bestselling categories and reading habits provide valuable insights for tailoring marketing strategies and selecting content that resonates with each country.

While most markets are dominated by a primary language, increasing globalization and cultural diversity have elevated the presence of other languages, particularly English. By adapting to these shifts, authors can better connect with readers across the globe.

Chapter 6 - The art of self-publishing

When I decided to publish my books independently, bypassing traditional publishing houses, I entered a vast and complex world, one filled with challenges but also immense opportunities. Self-publishing gave me the freedom to choose my topics, timelines, and the way I wanted to present my books to the world. Thanks to online platforms like Amazon, I discovered it was possible to reach readers across the globe. In this chapter, I'll share the strategies and techniques that helped me succeed as an independent author.

Choosing the right platform

The first major decision was selecting the platform for publishing my books. Among the many available options, some of the most prominent self-publishing platforms include IngramSpark, Barnes & Noble Press, Amazon KDP (Kindle Direct Publishing), Apple Books, Google Play Books, and Kobo Writing Life. Here's an overview of their key features, advantages, and limitations to help authors find the best fit for their needs.

To start, I chose Amazon KDP for its visibility and ease of publishing in multiple formats (eBooks and print). Amazon also offers access to a massive global audience and provides useful tools for tracking sales and gathering feedback.

Each platform, of course, has its strengths. For instance, Kobo is particularly popular in French- and Japanese-speaking regions, while Google Play Books is an excellent choice for reaching Android users. After publishing my first few books on Amazon, I expanded to other platforms to maximize visibility. A multi-channel strategy allows me to avoid relying solely on one platform and diversifies my revenue streams.

Platform highlights

1. IngramSpark

IngramSpark is a comprehensive self-publishing platform with a strong focus on high-quality printing and global distribution.

- Advantages:

- **Extensive distribution**: as part of Ingram Content Group, one of the world's largest book distributors, books published through IngramSpark are readily accessible to bookstores, libraries, and international retailers.

- **Print quality**: offers advanced printing options, including hardcover formats and various sizes, making it ideal for illustrated, photography, and high-quality books.

- **Multiple formats**: Supports both eBook and print publishing, allowing authors to reach a broader audience.

- Disadvantages:
- **Complex interface**: the platform's interface and approval process can be daunting for new authors, requiring extra time to prepare files.

- **Ideal for**: authors seeking complete international distribution and willing to invest in a platform with advanced printing options.

2. Barnes & Noble Press
Barnes & Noble Press provides a user-friendly platform for self-publishing, especially for authors looking to tap into the U.S. market.

- Advantages:
- **Direct distribution**: books are sold directly through the Barnes & Noble website in both eBook and print formats.
- **Ease of use**: simple and intuitive, making it easy for authors to upload their books.
- **No publishing fees**: there are no upfront costs, making it accessible for authors on a budget.

- Disadvantages:
- **Limited distribution**: primarily focused on the U.S. market, with less reach compared to Amazon or IngramSpark.
- **Fewer marketing tools**: offers fewer promotional options compared to Amazon.

- **Ideal for**: authors targeting the U.S. market and seeking direct access to Barnes & Noble's readers.

3. Amazon KDP (Kindle Direct Publishing)

Amazon KDP is the world's most widely used self-publishing platform, offering direct access to Amazon's global store.

- Advantages:
- **Global reach**: books are available worldwide in both digital (Kindle) and print formats.
- **Print on demand**: eliminates the need for inventory by printing books as they're ordered.
- **Marketing tools**: features like Kindle Countdown Deals and Kindle Unlimited boost visibility.
- **No publishing fees**: free to publish, with Amazon taking a percentage of sales.

- Disadvantages:
- **I haven't found any so far.**

- **Ideal for**: authors looking for a quick way to publish and reach a large audience through the most popular online marketplace.

4. Apple Books

Apple Books is Apple's self-publishing platform, ideal for reaching readers on iOS devices.

- Advantages:
- **Dedicated audience**: leverages Apple's loyal customer base.
- **Ease of use**: intuitive process for uploading eBooks.
- **No publishing fees**: free to publish on the platform.

- Disadvantages:
- **Limited distribution**: exclusively for iOS users, which excludes non-Apple audiences.
- **No print option**: only supports digital books.

- **Ideal for**: authors targeting Apple users and interested in digital-only formats.

5. Google Play Books
Google Play Books offers global eBook distribution via the Google Play Store, accessible on Android devices.

- Advantages:
- **Global reach**: integrated with Google Play, reaching readers worldwide.
- **Device accessibility**: accessible on Android devices and web browsers.
- **No publishing fees**: free to publish.

- Disadvantages:
- **Less intuitive interface**: can be harder to navigate compared to Amazon or Barnes & Noble.
- **Fewer promotional tools**: limited marketing features compared to Amazon.

- **Ideal for**: authors targeting Android users and a global audience.

6. Kobo Writing Life
Kobo Writing Life is the self-publishing arm of Kobo, with strong markets in Canada, Europe, and Asia.

- Advantages:
- **International distribution**: particularly strong in Canada, Europe, and Asia.
- **Local partnerships**: collaborates with local bookstores for wider reach.
- **No publishing fees**: free to use.

- Disadvantages:
- **Smaller U.S. market share**: less presence in the U.S. compared to Amazon or Barnes & Noble.
- **Fewer marketing tools**: limited promotional features.

- **Ideal for**: authors targeting international markets, especially in Canada and Europe.

Secret 11: diversify your platforms

Start with a single platform to familiarize yourself with the publishing process and understand the industry dynamics. Once you're comfortable and publishing multiple titles annually, consider expanding to other platforms. Diversifying ensures broader reach and reduces reliance on any one marketplace. Remember, each platform performs better in certain regions, and many readers remain loyal to their preferred platform. Focusing on one alone risks excluding potential buyers.

Formats and book presentation

Offering multiple formats is crucial. For instance, Amazon allows both eBooks and print via its Print on Demand service. This flexibility lets me cater to readers who prefer physical books as well as those who favor digital formats.

Secret 12: offer multiple formats

Over time, experiment with different book formats, varying page counts and sizes. Some readers prefer compact, straightforward books, while others value lengthy, content-rich editions.

Book presentation

When I publish a book, I ensure that the formatting is flawless. A well-formatted eBook that is easy to read and free of layout errors significantly enhances the reader's experience. The same applies to the print version, which must be well-designed and polished. I use Word for writing and layout and adhere to platform guidelines to avoid display issues.

Secret 13: the importance of the final check

Once the book is uploaded to the platform, resist the

urge to rush into printing. Most platforms provide a preview of the final product, showing how it will appear in print. Take a few minutes for this final check, it's a valuable time investment to ensure that minor errors, often caused by haste, don't make their way into the final version of your book.

The importance of an eye-catching cover

The cover is the first element that grabs reader's attention and is often decisive in convincing them to purchase a book. I quickly learned that a well-designed cover can make the difference between a book that goes unnoticed and one that captures interest. For this reason, I invest time (and money) in creating professional covers.

There are numerous resources for designing book covers: you can use tools like Canva, which are ideal for beginners, or collaborate with professional designers. Personally, I rely on a designer for all my book covers, choosing to work on platforms like [Fiverr](http://www.fiverr.com). On Fiverr, you can find hundreds of professionals who create high-quality covers that perfectly meet bookstore standards.

Creating the cover

Here's how the practical process of designing a book cover unfolds:

1. Choose the base image: once you've selected a designer, they'll send you a link to a stock image website where you can choose an image that best represents your book. Share this image with the designer.

2. Provide cover examples: send a few examples of book

covers you like that align with your desired style. For instance, I explore Amazon or other book retail sites to study the covers of bestsellers in my book's genre. This is an excellent way to create a cover that meets audience expectations.

Pay close attention to these first two steps, as they are essential to achieving a great result.

3. Book details: provide the designer with the following information: title, subtitle, author name, and back cover text. For the back of the book, I usually include a short summary (often created with the help of AI) and a brief author biography.

By following these steps, you can achieve a professional and eye-catching cover that enhances the value of your book.

Secret 14: outsource the cover design (even if you're a designer)

Delegate the creation of your book cover to an external professional. With a small investment, you can achieve outstanding, competitive results in a short time, so impressive that they'll rival the covers of major publishers. I assure you, readers won't notice any difference between your cover and those by authors who spend significant sums on signature designs.

Additionally, the time you save can be devoted to writing new books, thereby increasing your earnings and productivity.

Optimizing your title and description

Another essential element for a book's success is optimizing its title and description. The title must be clear, engaging, and immediately understandable, while the description should entice readers to learn more. In many cases, I've chosen titles that include specific keywords to help readers find my books through search features on sales platforms.

To create impactful titles, I conduct research on major book-selling sites, studying the titles of bestsellers in the subject I want to address. This allows me to draw inspiration from formulas that have already proven successful and to identify the most effective keywords for attracting an audience.

The description serves as a kind of "preview" of the book's content. It should be compelling and informative without giving too much away. I often start with a question that grabs attention, then explain in a few sentences why my book can be valuable to the reader.

Secret 15: tailor titles to markets

Adjust titles for different markets. Literal translations may not resonate as well as culturally tailored versions that speak directly to local audiences.

Choosing categories and keywords

One of the most effective strategies for increasing a book's visibility is to carefully select categories and keywords. Every platform allows you to choose specific categories and include keywords that help readers find your book. This step requires thorough research: it's essential to understand which categories are more competitive and which ones might offer better chances for visibility.

For example, if I publish a self-help book on productivity, I could place it in the "Personal Growth" or "Time Management" category. However, there might be a less competitive category, like "Career Development," that could provide greater visibility. Similarly, keywords must be chosen thoughtfully to match the search terms most commonly used by readers.

Promoting your book

Publishing a book is only the beginning; promotion is essential to make it known and drive sales. Initially, I focused on social media, sharing posts about my books and encouraging friends and acquaintances to support me. Over time, however, I discovered more effective marketing strategies, such as paid advertising and collaborations with industry influencers.

Amazon KDP, for instance, offers an advertising service that allows you to sponsor your book directly on the platform. This service has helped me reach readers who were previously unaware of my work and increase the visibility of my titles. I also run targeted ad campaigns on Facebook, aimed at specific audiences interested in the topics of my books.

Additionally, I started collaborating with bloggers and

influencers in my niche. Offering free copies in exchange for reviews has been a technique that helped me build a loyal readership and generate word-of-mouth. Positive reviews are crucial: they enhance the book's credibility and encourage new readers to take the next step and make a purchase.

Why advertise my books?

Amazon offers a unique opportunity to reach your audience right where they spend their time: shopping, reading, listening, or watching content. With sponsored ads, you can connect directly with readers through advertisements visible in Amazon's search results, promoting not only your books but also your brand as an author.

Here are some compelling statistics that highlight the effectiveness of Amazon Ads:

- 74% of shoppers remember seeing an ad during their visit to Amazon.

- 51% use Amazon in the early stages of their purchasing journey to research and discover new books.

- Shoppers who browse Amazon consider 22% more titles on average compared to those who don't.

- 46% of Amazon shoppers rely on search results to decide which books to purchase.

These numbers underscore the importance of being visible on the platform. Advertising your books allows you to boost visibility, reach new readers, and maximize your sales potential.

The importance of monitoring and adapting

Every book is an experiment. After publication, I consistently monitor sales and reader feedback to understand what works and what doesn't. Reviews, both positive and negative, are invaluable for improving the quality of my books and adjusting my strategy.

I analyze sales data to determine whether my advertising campaigns are effective and if the chosen categories and keywords are working as intended. If a book isn't performing as well as I hoped, I make adjustments: revising the description, experimenting with a new cover, or retargeting my ad campaigns.

Self-publishing a book requires careful planning, attention to detail, and ongoing effort. Every step, from choosing the platform to designing the cover, crafting the title, and promoting the book, can mean the difference between a book that goes unnoticed and one that achieves success.

Self-publishing has taught me to be not just an author but also a marketer and entrepreneur, capable of managing every stage of the process. This chapter is a practical guide for anyone embarking on the self-publishing journey. With the right strategies, it's possible to turn your work into a success and reach a wide, diverse audience.

Self-publishing isn't just an opportunity to write books; it's an opportunity to build an independent career, where every book becomes a small investment in yourself.

Chapter 7 - Promoting and marketing your book

Publishing a book is just the beginning of the journey. Once your book is available online, the next step is ensuring it gets noticed by as many people as possible, and convincing them to buy it. In this chapter, I'll share the strategies I've learned to effectively promote my books using a mix of social media, paid advertising, and reader engagement techniques.

Developing a marketing strategy

First and foremost, it's crucial to have a clear marketing strategy. Publishing a book without a plan to promote it is like tossing a message in a bottle into the sea, it might reach someone, but it's more likely to get lost. A well-thought-out marketing strategy can mean the difference between a book that sells only a handful of copies and one that becomes a true success.

For every book, I start by creating a detailed marketing plan. This includes specific goals, like the number of copies I want to sell in the first month, and the actions I'll take to promote the book. For example, I outline which advertising channels I'll invest in, which social media platforms I'll use for organic promotion, and which collaborations I'll pursue. This roadmap keeps me focused and helps me track the results of my efforts.

Each book requires a unique approach. Sometimes, I write a book as an "experiment" to test a new topic or market in a specific country. In these cases, I launch a general advertising campaign after publication to gauge the audience's reaction. Other times, when I have a clear understanding of the target niche, I focus on highly targeted ad campaigns. Keeping track of what works and what doesn't is essential for learning and improving over time. Experimentation is key, and everyone should build their knowledge step by step.

Secret 16: invest in advertising

Books don't sell themselves, especially your first ones. It's essential to allocate a budget for advertising. Over time, as your name becomes recognized and you build a solid base of loyal readers, each new publication will generate sales from the start.

Leveraging social media

Social media is a powerful tool for reaching new readers. Platforms like Facebook, Instagram, and even LinkedIn offer opportunities to connect directly with people and showcase your books. The key to success on social media is creating engaging content tailored to your target audience.

Instead of simply sharing a link to my book, I create posts that tell the story behind its creation, share excerpts to spark curiosity, and answer readers' questions. The goal is to build a relationship with my audience, making them feel connected to my creative process. Readers who feel personally invested in an author are more likely to support them by purchasing their books.

I also use Instagram and Facebook Stories for quick updates and short videos. Stories allow me to interact more casually and directly with readers. I include polls, questions, and behind-the-scenes content to keep the engagement high.

The power of paid advertising

Paid advertising campaigns are an effective way to increase a book's visibility and reach new readers. Platforms like Amazon, Facebook, and Google Ads provide targeted options to promote your book to specific audiences based on their interests and behaviors.

I always start with Amazon Advertising, which allows me to sponsor my book directly on the platform. Sponsored books appear in search results and on the pages of similar titles, increasing their visibility to readers already in a buying mindset.

Facebook Ads is another valuable tool. With Facebook, I can create visually appealing ads targeting specific demographics such as age, interests, and location. This helps me reach the exact type of reader likely to be interested in my book. For instance, for a book about productivity, I target professionals, entrepreneurs, and college students.

Collaborating with influencers and bloggers

Partnering with influencers and bloggers in your book's niche can significantly boost visibility and sales. I've reached out to niche bloggers and social media influencers, offering them a free copy of my book in exchange for an honest review or a mention.

Collaborations with influencers can have a huge impact because their followers often trust their recommendations. If the influencer finds value in my book, it's likely that their audience will as well. This strategy also generates word-of-mouth marketing, one of the most effective forms of promotion.

Secret 17: the power of collaborations

Take the time to find influencers in your book's niche. Some books have become bestsellers simply because they were promoted by the right influencer.

Offering free excerpts and temporary promotions

A great way to attract new readers is by offering free excerpts or running limited-time promotions. Many self-publishing platforms, like Amazon KDP, allow you to offer discounted or free books for a short period. I've experimented with this strategy for some of my titles and found that increased visibility during promotions often leads to higher sales even after the promotion ends.

Sharing a free excerpt on social media or my website is another effective approach. By giving readers a taste of the content, I can spark their interest and encourage them to purchase the full book.

Building a mailing list

A mailing list is one of the most valuable tools in book marketing. Having a list of readers interested in my books allows me to promote new releases, offer exclusive discounts, and maintain a direct connection with my audience.

To grow my mailing list, I offer free content on my website, like excerpts or bonus materials, in exchange for email addresses. I use this list to keep readers informed about upcoming projects and promotions, always aiming to provide value rather than just pushing sales. A well-maintained mailing list fosters reader loyalty and boosts the chances of repeat purchases.

Engaging with readers and gathering feedback

Direct engagement with readers is a cornerstone of my marketing strategy. I encourage readers to leave reviews on sales platforms and thank them publicly for their support. If someone sends me a comment via email or social media, I always respond to show my appreciation.

Reader reviews are vital for building a book's reputation. They're often the first thing potential buyers look at before making a purchase decision. By fostering a connection with readers, I not only improve my books but also create a community that supports my work.

Monitoring results and adapting

Finally, tracking the results of marketing efforts is essential to understanding what works and what doesn't. I use analytics tools from advertising platforms and sales dashboards to monitor book sales, ad performance, and promotional success. Based on these insights, I adjust my strategies to focus on the most effective techniques.

Book marketing is a dynamic process that requires continuous experimentation and fine-tuning. Sometimes a strategy that worked for one book may not be as effective for the next. By carefully monitoring data and adapting my approach, I ensure my books remain visible and maximize their sales potential.

Promoting a book takes dedication, creativity, and patience. Publishing alone doesn't guarantee success; you need to actively work to get your book noticed and attract new readers. The techniques I've shared in this chapter have helped me build a strong presence as an author and foster a loyal reader base.

Book marketing is a mix of strategy and authenticity. When you work with passion and build genuine relationships with your audience, success will follow. Promotion is an investment in yourself and your projects, with the potential to turn your book into a true audience favorite.

Chapter 8 - The life of a successful writer

Achieving success as a writer has profoundly transformed my life. Looking back, I barely recognize the person I was when I started this journey. I had a steady but ordinary job, a life dictated by predictable routines, and a hidden dream that seemed too far-fetched. I never imagined that one day I would sell 100,000 books and earn the freedom to travel, write, and live life on my terms. In this chapter, I want to share how my daily life has changed and what it means to live as a successful writer today.

Freedom and flexibility

One of the most significant changes has been the ability to work from anywhere, at any time. Today, I can wake up in a remote corner of the world or a city I've always dreamed of visiting and start writing with nothing more than my laptop. No longer tied to an office or fixed hours, my life now strikes a balance between freedom and creativity.

Being a digital writer allows me to travel without constraints and choose where to live at any moment. I often spend months in one city, immersing myself in local life, and then move to another country when it feels like the right time to find new inspiration. This flexibility has reshaped how I view the world, with every place now offering potential ideas for my books.

Writing as a way of life

Writing has become not just a job but a lifestyle. Wherever I go, I carry the desire to tell stories, share insights, and explore new ideas. It's not just about creating new books but about observing the world with curiosity and seeking stories in the people I meet and the landscapes I encounter. I've learned that writing requires openness—a readiness to embrace inspiration, even in the most unexpected moments.

When I visit new places, I focus on how people live, their dreams, and their struggles. I love immersing myself in local cultures, learning new customs, and savoring different cuisines. These experiences enrich my books, giving them greater depth and authenticity. I believe a writer must live fully to convey genuine emotions, and my life today revolves around that principle.

Managing success and finances

Being a successful writer also means learning to manage finances responsibly. Despite earning well from book sales, I've chosen to maintain a balanced and thoughtful approach. One of the first lessons I learned was the importance of planning for the future, investing wisely, and building a safety net. While the writer's life can seem adventurous, financial stability is crucial.

Today, I can afford to live comfortably, travel, and enjoy

my time, but I've also learned to invest part of my earnings in projects or opportunities that offer long-term returns. This balance between freedom and responsibility enables me to grow as a writer while maintaining the security I need to explore new projects without worry.

Secret 18: plan for stability, not just the moment

Success can be fleeting, and it's not always guaranteed to last. Avoid drastically changing your lifestyle or spending recklessly. Instead, focus on sustainability. Consider intelligent investment strategies that can generate steady income, ensuring financial security even if initial success wanes. Planning ahead today can safeguard your well-being tomorrow.

Relationships and personal time

One of the most rewarding aspects of success is having the time to nurture important relationships. The life of a writer can be solitary, but success has given me the freedom to choose when to be alone and when to surround myself with people.

Quality time has become essential to me. I've learned to respect my own rhythms, to step back from work when I'm not inspired, and to take the time I need to recharge. Every day is a choice, a balance between work and personal life, which has allowed me to grow both as a person and as an author.

New challenges and future projects

Success has opened doors to new projects and opportunities I never imagined. Today, I can afford to write purely for pleasure, exploring topics that fascinate me, even if they're not "commercial." I have the freedom to dive into creative endeavors, such as writing short stories or experimenting with new genres, without worrying too much about financial returns.

I'm also considering ways to share my experience with others. I'd love to help emerging writers find their paths by creating courses or content that guides them through self-publishing and marketing. I firmly believe that success is most meaningful when shared, and helping others achieve their goals would be a way to give back.

Living in the present moment

One of the most valuable lessons I've learned is the importance of living in the present moment. Traveling and writing have taught me that every moment is unique and irreplaceable, and time is the most precious resource we have. I strive to make the most of each day, to live authentically, and to center my life around my passions.

Being a writer has led me to deeply reflect on what it means to live a fulfilling life. It's not just about achieving goals or accumulating successes but about building a life where every moment is an opportunity to grow, learn, and create. Today, I feel truly free and fulfilled, and that is the greatest gift writing has given me.

The life of a successful writer is about more than recognition and financial rewards; it's about choices, freedom, and authenticity. Every day is an opportunity to reinvent yourself, discover new aspects of who you are, explore the world, and find inspiration. This chapter is an invitation to anyone dreaming of turning their passion into a livelihood: never stop believing in yourself and in the possibility of building a life that's authentic, free, and meaningful.

Being a writer is a constant evolution. Looking back, I'm grateful for every step of this journey. I've learned that true success lies in living the way I want, making writing the center of my life, and finding peace in being myself.

Chapter 9 - Overcoming criticism and managing success

Being a successful writer brings immense satisfaction, but it also comes with challenges, facing criticism, judgment, and high expectations that can sometimes be difficult to navigate. When I first started publishing, I never imagined that alongside praise, I would also encounter criticism and negative feedback. Learning to balance success with a resilient and grounded mindset became an essential part of my journey. In this chapter, I'll share the strategies that have helped me handle criticism and manage the emotions tied to recognition.

Embracing criticism as part of the journey

When I published my first books, positive reviews filled me with pride, while negative ones hit me hard. A single bad comment could make me doubt my abilities as a writer and shake my confidence. Over time, however, I came to understand that every book is subject to criticism, and this feedback is an inevitable part of every author's growth.

Accepting criticism was one of the most important lessons I learned. I've come to view it not as a personal attack but as a variety of opinions that can help me improve. Every reader has different expectations, preferences, and tastes; I cannot expect everyone to love my work. Today, I distinguish between constructive criticism, which I embrace and use to refine my skills, and destructive criticism, which I let go of as part of the inevitable "noise" that accompanies public writing.

Learning from constructive feedback

Some of the most valuable insights I've gained have come from readers offering specific suggestions to improve my books. Initially, it wasn't easy to accept these suggestions, but over time, I realized that listening to feedback is an opportunity to grow and create better content. I now regularly review comments, especially those that provide actionable advice. Sometimes these are simple suggestions, such as stylistic tweaks or the addition of more examples, but they can make a significant difference to the final product.

Feedback has also helped me understand my audience better. By reading reviews, I've learned what readers appreciate and what they hope to see in my future works. This connection with my audience allows me to build a genuine relationship and create content that resonates with their needs and desires.

Handling destructive criticism

Not all criticism is constructive. Unfortunately, being a writer also exposes you to destructive comments, ones that are often baseless and meant to discourage rather than help. I've received reviews that seemed intent on diminishing my work, offering no useful feedback. Early on, these criticisms destabilized me, making me question my path. But with time, I've learned how to handle them.

I've realized that while I can't control what people say about me or my books, I can control how I respond. Today, I approach destructive criticism with detachment: I read it, acknowledge it, and then let it go. I don't allow it to impact my self-esteem or creativity. Every author faces similar criticisms, and I've come to see them as a natural part of public exposure.

Maintaining a balanced perspective on success

Success can be a double-edged sword. On one hand, it brings recognition and satisfaction; on the other, it can create pressure and heightened expectations. When my first book achieved significant success, I felt compelled to replicate it and continue meeting readers' expectations. This pressure occasionally threatened to overshadow my creativity and take the joy out of writing.

To avoid falling into this trap, I've learned to maintain a balanced perspective. Success is important, but it doesn't define my worth as a person or as an author. Writing is my passion, and my primary goal is to continue creating content that excites me. If one book doesn't perform as well as the last, that's okay, every project has its own path and audience.

Celebrating milestones and recognizing progress

One of the most important lessons I've learned is the value of celebrating every milestone, big or small. Selling

100,000 copies was a remarkable achievement, but each book I've published is a success in its own right. Celebrating my progress allows me to acknowledge my efforts and renew my motivation to keep writing.

It's easy to focus only on major achievements and overlook the small victories along the way. For me, taking the time to appreciate each step—whether it's a positive review, a heartfelt message from a reader, or completing a new project—has become essential. Each book is a building block in my career, and celebrating these moments gives me the energy to tackle challenges with greater resilience.

Building resilience and staying true to yourself

Being a successful writer requires resilience and a strong sense of self. External pressures, criticism, and expectations can be overwhelming, but I've learned that the key to navigating them is staying true to myself. I write because I love it, because I want to share ideas and inspire others. I don't let others' opinions dictate my journey or cloud my vision.

Cultivating resilience has helped me develop an emotional armor that shields me from the highs and lows of public life. Every day, I strive to improve, grow as an author, and remain committed to my values. This commitment to myself serves as my compass, reminding me that beyond criticism and success, my passion for writing is what drives every decision I make.

Turning challenges into growth opportunities

Overcoming criticism and managing success are challenges that every author faces, but they also present opportunities for personal growth. I've learned to see criticism as a tool for improvement, to build a support network, and to maintain a balanced perspective on success. Each day, I remind myself that my worth isn't defined by a single book or review but by the passion and dedication I bring to my work.

This chapter is an invitation to all authors, both aspiring and established, not to be discouraged by difficulties or others' opinions. Writing is a journey, and every step teaches us something new about ourselves and the world around us. By continuing to write with resilience and authenticity, we can embrace the challenges and fully experience the life of a writer.

Chapter 10 - Mistakes to avoid and lessons learned

My journey as a writer has been filled with mistakes and lessons that have shaped me both personally and professionally. Each misstep taught me something valuable, helping me refine my approach and improve my craft. In this chapter, I want to share some of the errors I made in hopes that they might help others starting out on their own path. Avoiding common pitfalls and learning from the experiences of others can make a significant difference.

1. Underestimating the importance of quality

When I first began publishing books, I focused primarily on quantity, believing that building a large catalog quickly would boost my overall sales. However, I soon realized that quality far outweighs quantity. Rushing to publish books without ensuring high standards can lead to negative reviews and damage your reputation as an author.

I've learned that every book must be thoughtfully planned, well-structured, and meticulously polished. Quality shows in every aspect, writing, formatting, cover design, and final edits. A reader who enjoys one book is more likely to read others from the same author, while a disappointed reader will rarely return. Today, I dedicate more time to each book, ensuring it meets my standards before releasing it.

2. Overlooking the importance of editing

Early on, I was tempted to skip the editing process or rely solely on basic automated corrections. I assumed this would be enough to ensure readability, but I quickly realized that editing is a critical step in the writing process. Small errors, inconsistencies, or unclear sentences can easily slip through and disrupt the reader's experience.

Now, I always conduct a thorough final review to ensure that every word is in its proper place. While this process requires time and patience, it's an investment that pays off. A well-edited book conveys professionalism and respect for the reader.

3. Skipping market research

One of my early mistakes was choosing topics based solely on my personal interests without considering whether there was an actual market for them. On several occasions, I published books on niche subjects that had little demand or audience interest. This resulted in low sales and frustration, as my efforts didn't yield the rewards I had hoped for.

I've since learned that market research is essential. Before writing a book, I now ensure there's an interested audience and potential for sales. I explore Amazon categories, analyze trends, and read reviews of similar books to understand what readers are looking for. This helps me make more strategic decisions and focus on topics with greater chances of success.

4. Neglecting the cover and title

The cover and title are critical elements of a book's success. They often determine whether a book grabs a reader's attention or fades into obscurity. A well-designed cover and a compelling title can make all the difference.

For cover design, I always work with professional graphic designers. While DIY options may seem cost-effective, they can result in subpar designs that fail to compete in the marketplace. The cover serves as a book's "business card" and must visually communicate its essence, capturing readers' attention immediately.

Similarly, the title is a crucial factor. A great title should be clear, evocative, and include relevant keywords. It's not uncommon for a book to be chosen solely because its title piques a reader's curiosity or stirs emotion. I now dedicate time to studying successful titles in my genre for inspiration and to craft something unique and engaging.

5. Trying to do everything alone

For a long time, I tried to handle everything on my own, writing, editing, cover design, and promotion. I wanted to save money and felt capable of managing all aspects of self-publishing. However, I soon realized that being an author requires specialized skills and that doing everything alone can lead to lower quality and unnecessary stress.

Today, I collaborate with professionals for certain stages of the process, such as editing and cover design. This allows me to focus on writing and ensures a more polished final product. Learning to delegate has been one of the most valuable lessons, recognizing your limits and trusting experts can elevate a book from mediocre to exceptional.

6. Underestimating marketing and promotion

Another early mistake was underestimating the importance of marketing and promotion. I would publish my books and hope readers would find them on their own, without dedicating time to actively promote them. This approach proved ineffective in a highly competitive industry, where even the best books need visibility.

Now, I see marketing as an integral part of being an author. I invest in advertising, leverage social media, collaborate with bloggers and influencers, and run targeted promotions. Marketing isn't an "extra" but a necessary component to reach readers. Without a promotional strategy, it's difficult to stand out and achieve the recognition your books deserve.

7. Ignoring reader feedback

Initially, I focused solely on my vision and goals, paying little attention to reader feedback and requests. This attitude caused me to miss valuable opportunities, as readers provide insights and inspiration that can help improve and refine your work.

Today, I actively listen to my readers. I respond to their messages, read reviews, and try to understand what they appreciate and expect from my books. This helps me build genuine connections and create a community that follows my journey. Readers are at the heart of my work, and giving them a voice adds value to everything I create.

8. Letting fear of failure hold you back

A psychological mistake I made early on was letting the fear of failure paralyze me. Each time I published a book, I worried it might not resonate, sell poorly, or receive negative reviews. This fear often hindered my creativity and willingness to experiment.

Over time, I've learned that failure is part of growth and that every experience, whether successful or not—is an opportunity to improve. Now, I approach each new publication with curiosity and openness, without fearing judgment. My goal is continuous improvement, and I know every misstep brings me closer to becoming a better writer.

Mistakes are inevitable on any journey, but the ability to learn from them is what makes the difference between temporary setbacks and lasting success. Every error has taught me valuable lessons, helping me hone my skills and grow as an author. This chapter is an invitation to anyone dreaming of a writing career to embrace mistakes as a natural part of the learning process.

I'm grateful for every experience, as they've helped me build a solid foundation and cultivate an open, resilient mindset. The key is not to be discouraged and to keep improving, step by step. I hope the lessons I've shared can serve as a guide for those who, like me, have chosen to follow their passion and turn it into a career.

Chapter 11 - Final advice and inspiration for aspiring writers

Reaching the end of this book means we've explored the journey that led me to become a successful writer, from choosing the right topics to handling criticism and learning from mistakes. But the message I want to leave with you goes beyond techniques and strategies. Writing is a journey, and true success comes not just from sales or recognition but from passion, perseverance, and the courage to pour yourself into every word. This chapter is dedicated to everyone who dreams of embarking on this adventure, with final advice and words of inspiration to turn the dream of writing into reality.

1. Start Now, don't wait for perfection

One of the biggest obstacles for many writers is the quest for perfection. They wait for the perfect idea, the perfect sentence, or the ideal conditions to start. The truth is, perfection doesn't exist. Start now, with what you have and with the ideas that inspire you today. Writing is a process, and every book will teach you something new. Don't be afraid to begin with an idea that feels small or imperfect; often, what matters most is taking that first step. Only by walking the path will you discover where it leads.

2. Cultivate consistency

Consistency is the key to transforming passion into a career. Writing requires dedication, and building a routine will help keep the creative process alive. Find a rhythm that works for you, whether it's writing daily or dedicating specific hours each week to your project. The important thing is to stay consistent. Even on days when the words don't come easily, sit down and try to write something. Consistency builds discipline, and discipline is what will carry you through to the completion of your book.

3. Read and learn from the best

Reading is an endless source of inspiration and learning. Explore books from different genres, established authors, and emerging talents to discover a variety of styles and perspectives. Pay attention to what you admire in other writers' works: how they develop characters, structure sentences, and pace their stories. Learning from the best will help you develop your own voice and grow as a writer. Reading opens your mind and provides ideas that you can adapt and make your own.

4. Listen to your readers, but stay true to yourself

Readers are a valuable resource; they are the heart of a writer's audience. Take time to listen to their feedback, respond to their messages and reviews, and understand what they appreciate in your books. However, remain true to yourself and your vision. Don't write just to please an audience or chase trends, write what genuinely excites you. Authenticity creates connection, and readers can tell when a book is written with passion and sincerity.

5. Experiment and step outside your comfort zone

Every writer has a preferred style and favorite topics, but experimenting is essential for growth. Try different genres, explore new subjects, and don't be afraid to take risks. You might discover a new passion or a dimension of your writing you hadn't considered. Let yourself be inspired, and don't hesitate to leave your comfort zone. Every new writing experience is an opportunity to evolve and surprise yourself. Sometimes, the best ideas come from unexpected places.

6. Embrace lifelong learning

The world of writing and publishing is constantly changing. New technologies, platforms, and methods are reshaping the literary landscape. Stay curious and open to learning. Explore digital tools, experiment with artificial intelligence, and use social media to connect with your readers. A commitment to continuous learning will keep you ahead of the curve and help you seize emerging opportunities.

7. Accept failure as part of the journey

Not every book will be a success. Not every idea will work as expected. Failure is an inevitable part of every writer's journey, but it shouldn't discourage you. Every misstep is an opportunity to learn and improve. I've published books that didn't achieve the results I hoped for, but they pushed me to do better, rethink my strategies, and keep writing. Embrace failure as a lesson in growth, and never stop believing in your worth.

8. Find joy in writing beyond success

While writing can become a career, it should never lose its element of joy and inspiration. Find happiness in the act of writing, even when things don't go as planned. Success is rewarding, but the true motivation for the long term is your passion for stories, words, and the message you want to share. Every time you write, remember why you started, the desire to express what's inside you. The greatest satisfaction comes from knowing that through writing, you're creating something unique.

9. Cultivate patience and perseverance

Becoming a successful writer isn't an overnight achievement. It requires patience, perseverance, and the ability to navigate difficult moments. There will be days when sales are slow, when you feel stuck, or when progress seems elusive. But writing is a marathon, not a sprint. Cultivate patience and keep working with dedication. Perseverance will help you overcome obstacles and build a solid, lasting career.

10. Let your unique voice shine

The most important advice I can give is to let your authentic voice shine through. Every writer has something unique to say, a perspective no one else can offer. Your voice is what sets you apart and makes your books special. Don't try to imitate others or be afraid of standing out. Find your authenticity and let it flow into your words.

Readers crave authenticity, and when you write with honesty, you create a connection that transcends the page.

This book was written as a guide to help aspiring writers navigate their path to success, but it's also an invitation to follow your passion and believe in your abilities. Writing is an act of courage and creativity, a process that demands dedication and effort. But it's also one of the most rewarding and profound experiences you can have.

If you're reading this, it means you have the desire to write, to create, to share your voice with the world. Don't let challenges hold you back. Remember, every great writer began with a blank page and a vision. Nurture that vision, keep learning, stay resilient, and write with passion. Success will come, but what truly matters is the journey you build with every book, every word.

Go forward, write, and tell your story. The world needs authentic voices, stories that inspire, and words that touch hearts. You are ready to be one of those storytellers.

www.ingramcontent.com/pod-product-compliance
Lightning Source LLC
Chambersburg PA
CBHW052335220526
45472CB00001B/438